IDENTITY CRISIS

Reclaiming the Authority of our Spirit through God

Overseer Sandra D. Carter

Vision of Breath with Life Ministries

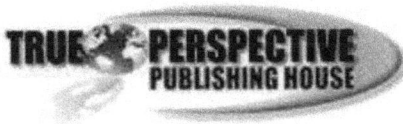

TRUE PERSPECTIVE PUBLISHING HOUSE

Foreword

Author and Overseer Sandra D. Carter is our present-day wonder woman. She has a heart of gold and a passion for teaching. She trains daily on the spiritual battlefield interceding for the world. Her profound honesty in *Identity Crisis: Reclaiming the Authority of our Spirit through God* provides the reader with a superpower kit of basic biblical and practical points about our identity in Christ.

It stirs your heart and empowers you to read the Word of God. My desire to read Overseer Carter's book in one sitting intensified chapter after chapter. While reading chapter two, "Looking in the Mirror," I asked myself, "When you look in the mirror what do you see?" You can look in the mirror every day and certainly not see yourself. Chapter four, "We are more than a Conqueror (Check your DNA)," boldly tells you that if you want to know who you are, and whose you are, you do not have to search a DNA website. *Identity Crisis* will guide you to wonder no more. It is a page turner that causes you to look deep into your soul. It gives hope to the hopeless and life to anyone who feels like giving up. Overseer Carter shares her personal testimony on how God changed her life through trials she endured as a pastor.

Your life will be transformed by Overseer Carter's teachings on how God sees you as a person through His Word. You will never view people or yourself in the same way after you learn the steps of knowing who you are in God through biblical truth. Buckle up and get ready for a spiritual breakthrough and a revelation of your true identity!

Alicia S. Jones, Motivational Speaker and Author of Sentenced to Live

Acknowledgements

I give honor and praise to God and my Lord and Savior Jesus Christ for giving me the wisdom and spiritual understanding through the Holy Spirit to write this book. Our identity in Christ is precious because He sacrificed His life for us on the cross so that we might be filled with all the fullness of God. Through Christ, we have overcome the adversity and evil that is in the world, and we are no longer ensnared in the bondage of an identity crisis.

I thank my family in Columbus, Ohio and Richmond, Virginia for their prayers, support and encouragement. I also thank the disciples in my church in Columbus, Vision of Breath with Life Ministries, for their perseverance in coming out to hear the Word of God and learning how to apply Scripture in their lives. A special thanks to Jessica A. Johnson who diligently worked with me on this project from the beginning. I also appreciate Shawmeen Henderson and Kim Estes for assisting me with editing my book chapters and Mioshi Oglesby for drawing my sketches.

I pray that as you read *Identity Crisis* that you will seek the Lord Jesus Christ with your whole heart and come to know who you truly are in Him. May the grace and peace of God richly bless you!

Table of Contents

Introduction

We are living in a time of chaos where many of us are stressed out. The church is going through an identity crisis through the Spirit, and the world is looking at us in an entirely different manner regarding our faith. This is why I wanted to introduce the crisis in the believer and also let unbelievers know that they are from God too. We all have God's DNA.

That is how we got here. It started with our human spirit, and I believe this is the key to experiencing Christ and living a victorious Christian life. As a Christian myself, I wrote this book because of the misunderstanding of God's Word by many people, and I wanted to share that Jesus Christ is an amazing and wonderful person within us. We received forgiveness for our sins through Christ's death on the cross and are delivered from God's eternal judgment.

Jesus came to live in the deepest part of our human spirit as our Savior so that we can enjoy our lives with Him. Genesis 2:7 says, "And the LORD God formed man *of* the dust of the ground, and breathed into his nostrils the breath of life; and man became a living soul." We can see that

God made us with a human spirit and that our physical body was made from the dust of the ground. Our living soul is the psychological seat of the mind, emotions and will. Proverbs 20:27 states that the "spirit of a man *is* the lamp of the Lord, Searching all the inner depths of his heart" (New King James Version). The "inner depths" represent the wholeness of man. This is why we need understanding of God's Word and why Jesus shed His blood for us on the cross.

Do not just settle for having your name on a church roll membership. Know who you are spiritually in the Lord and know that the deepest part of your being was created by God. It is time to receive the SPIRITUAL DNA that has to come through God, who is the Head of our lives. We must know His Word to follow the SPIRITUAL DNA and to know our calling that God has put in us. The only way we can make a change is that we must believe we need a change. Do not forget that God is a Spirit, and He is coming back for our spirit, soul and body. They are very important, especially in this day and time.

As you read this book, you will learn that our human spirit is significant to God because He desires to abide within us. God wants us to receive Him. My spirit and your spirit are the receivers of life by knowing God. I often read John 3:6 where Jesus says, "That which is born of the flesh is flesh; and that which is born of the Spirit is spirit." The first Spirit is divine, which is the Holy Spirit of God, and the second spirit is the human spirit, which generates the soul of man.

The following are some key definitions that you will need to understand while reading this book.

Identity – the individual characteristic by which a thing or a person is recognized or known, it has attributes or traits.

DNA – your genetic code inherited from your parents, it includes traits that you share such as skin, hair and eye color.

Holy Spirit – the invisible, energizing force that God puts into action to accomplish His will.

Power – an inherent characteristic of God, it is the result of His nature.

Old man – it is an un-renewed man, the natural man who lives within the corruption of sin.

New man – it is the new creature or creation that we become once we receive the Holy Spirit who transforms us.

Soul – the part of man that enables him to think and reason, it cannot exist independently of the physical body; your inspiration, feelings, emotions, passions, thoughts, and your human spirit.

God – is our Creator of the heavens, earth and mankind, He is the Father of Jesus Christ.

Jesus – the Son of God, the one who died for our sins and laid His life down on the cross that we might have eternal life.

Satan – the adversary of God and man, he is the opposite of what God stands for.

Sin – the disobedience or rebellion against God that started with Adam and Eve, sin violates God's love.

Faith – complete trust or confidence in someone or something, a strong belief in God.

Christian – one who follows Christ, someone who is Christ-like.

Bible – the Word of God written by men who were inspired by the Holy Spirit.

Prayer – prayer is the ministry of the Word of God, which you use to take your petitions to Him; the Lord's Prayer is one of the greatest prayers you can use when you do not know what to say; you can find this prayer in Matthew 6:9-13.

Chapter One: What is our Identity Crisis?

Having been in church all of my life, I have asked myself how could I have an identity crisis if I am walking with the Lord? How could this be possible when you come from a church background and a Christian family? I really did not know about my spiritual DNA with the Lord or that He wanted to have a personal relationship with me. I always thought that when people mentioned church they were referring to a building. They seldom said that the church was in me because Christ is the Head of the church.

I grew up in a close-knit, black church community in Richmond, Virginia during the 1950s and 60s. My family was large, which was common in those days for blacks living in the South. I was the youngest of nine siblings, having three brothers and five sisters, and I reveled in getting all of the attention as the baby girl. My mother kept us in church and did the best she could to make sure – as the old folks used to say back then – that we "walked the straight and narrow." I never knew what the "straight and narrow" was because they did not talk about how Christ came in the human form to teach us about love. They did not explain that we are new creatures in Him and old things are passed away. The church was very strict about what we could and could not do. I heard more of what we could not do than about my spiritual DNA in God. Don't get me wrong. I am not trying to criticize the church. Many of the elders whom I sat under trusted God wholeheartedly by what they were taught, and I saw that God really helped

them. However, as a young person who had no clue regarding how I should walk in Christ, no one could answer the questions I had. Their answers were always "give it over to Jesus" or "just pray about it." That is what we went by. We prayed and sometimes I did get an answer, and I believe it was because I was sincere and in a crisis. This is why we had an identity crisis because we felt that we should go to church and repeat what the elders were doing, but they were getting by on what they believed and they did not fully know their identity in the Lord. Some went by church tradition and what they learned from their ministers or pastors. Many times it worked, and now I know that even through their lack of understanding God still moved in their lives. I later found out that this was based on their faith. They had strong faith. For example, a member's house could be burning down but they had faith and prayed that Jesus would work it out. And before you knew it, He did. I recognized that was God. It takes a lot of faith and prayer today for things to be worked out by Jesus Christ because He is supposed to be in us, and we should be walking with Him and reading His Word.

My family was in church because of my mother. She was the one who guided us to the Lord Jesus Christ. My mother would search around for churches that preached the truth so that we could know Christ as our personal Savior. She had steadfast faith in God that kept us going, especially when bills needed to be paid. My father used his money on other things instead of taking care of the household. He was the type who worked but never spent a lot of time with his children. He did his part occasionally, but my mother was the rock of our family and I can remember the many times my mother called prayer. We had to crawl out of our beds early in the morning. I mean EARLY. But those prayers helped us to have faith and trust in the Lord. There was one church that my mother really liked, and she always said, "They are really preaching the Word!" She believed this because she studied the Bible a lot, and she wrote songs and poems. She also played the guitar and the piano. She was all into God. As the youngest, I would have never thought we were not really following the fullness of God due to the things we did in church. For instance, my family sang and we had a small gospel group. I always enjoyed that, yet I did not realize that I was in an identity crisis because there is much more to serving God than just singing and attending Sunday morning services. I believed at that time that my mother would carry me to heaven. She prayed for me and taught us the Word, and sometimes I was not listening. I had brothers who were called to preach, but they were not living the way God wanted them to live. I am not judging them or anyone who is reading this book, but I want you to understand that we have a human DNA and a spiritual DNA. It is difficult to reach people for Christ today because we have been so used to following our human identity.

The pastors I was under when I was young did not teach or preach in depth about our identity in Christ. They talked about what we could not do – church rules and what they felt that Christ did not want us to do – instead of teaching us about our souls. Our crisis today is our soul, which houses our feelings and emotional makeup. Our soul is what sins, and we need the identity of Jesus Christ to get our soul on the right track.

Maybe you have a crisis in your life similar to the one I had where you have been in church for years but still do not know God on a personal level. Maybe you are just a babe in Christ and you feel overwhelmed by distressing circumstances or you did not completely surrender your all to the Lord. This is why I wanted to write this book because God has taught me about His identity through Jesus and the Holy Spirit. So, who is Jesus exactly? One of the most quoted Scriptures about Jesus is John 3:16, which says, "For God so loved the world, that he gave his only begotten Son, that whosoever believeth in him should not perish, but have everlasting life." However, there is so much more to Jesus than this Scripture. He wants a personal relationship with you. He wants to abide in you and instruct you to do some things that will be hard for you to bear, and when you do not have a servant's spirit you cannot follow Him. The crisis that we are talking about is when we do not know our identity in Christ and when we do not understand or have the wisdom of what God wants us to do. It is hard to be in a crisis with no understanding because it gets worse, and it is not good to live life without understanding.

If you follow Jesus, you will find out that His identity will lead you to the best life you have ever had! From my experience in church, I have seen many people just simply stop at a surface belief in Christ. I also did this because I did not ask God for wisdom and knowledge. Attending worship services and Bible study regularly, people try their best to live right, but when they slip up and make a mistake or sin, they feel extreme guilt about their shortcomings. Depending on the nature of their sin, some people actually begin to believe that God does not love them anymore and they stop coming to church, which is a crisis. They do not want to ask their pastor questions or talk about their situations and life challenges. I want to remind you that John 3:16 remains true. God still loves us! He just wants us to have His newfound identity.

The identity we were born in is sin. Romans 5:12 says, "Therefore, just as sin came into the world through one man, and death through sin, so death spread to all people [no one being able to stop it or escape its power], because they all sinned" (Amplified Bible). When we read the Scriptures, the seventh chapter of Romans talks about our struggles against sin, particularly with Moses' law and God's law. Moses' law fully exposed what was already in man's heart, and God's law (Ten Commandments) was the

law that He wanted us to keep. Moses' law brought to light the sin that was in the people.

In order for us to be able to keep God's law under grace, God sent His Son, Jesus. The Bible tells us in Galatians 3:13 that "Christ hath redeemed us from the curse of the law, being made a curse for us." When Jesus took our sins on the cross, His sacrificial death released us from the condemnation of sin through the law. We are now righteous in the sight of God and not guilty. We do not have to sin anymore! It is God who called us! Isn't that love? We could not call ourselves because we had no idea that we were in an identity crisis.

When we accept God's call, He changes our lives to become new creatures and old things are passed away, but the enemy, Satan, comes along and tries to steal what God has given us.

We can now go boldly to God's throne of grace because Jesus is our Mediator, and as our Savior and "High Priest" He has been "touched with the feeling of our infirmities; but was in all points tempted like as *we are, yet* without sin" (Hebrews 4:15). We do not have to be perfect, but our identity and way of life should be following the perfect man, who is Christ Jesus. We should meditate and study the Word of God. This enables us to have daily fellowship and communion with Him and establishes our Christian identity.

In Jesus' earthly ministry, it was evident that He wanted a relationship with those who believed. For example, in Luke 19 Jesus called Zacchaeus, a chief tax collector who was a wealthy man. Zacchaeus was of small stature and he could not get through the multitudes to see Jesus. Couldn't you imagine how frustrated he was? And he probably thought, *I'm rich. I should be able to get through the crowd.* Many people in church have felt this way when it seems hard to get to Jesus. They may say, "I pay my tithes and offering" or "I sing in the praise team and in the choir," but they still feel lost because they do not understand the identity of Christ. Have you ever felt like that? Let us pause for a moment and think about this. This is where some of us are right now, but look at how determined Zacchaeus was to see Jesus. He climbed up into a sycomore tree to watch Christ pass by. When Jesus got there He looked up, saw Zacchaeus, and told him, "Make haste, and come down; for to day I must abide at thy house" (Luke 19:5). God knows what His children need and often pulls out His grace in spite of their unbelief. People complained about Jesus befriending Zacchaeus because tax collectors were considered the worst of sinners, but Jesus was looking at the inward man. People often look on the outside first, having never considered one's inward man. Most of our crises are on the inside because of what we hear people say and what we see people do. We show it from the inside out and then people assume they know our identity.

We must trust the lead of God because trust leads to rewards. Lack of it can lead to loss. We need to fight through to make it through. Jesus wants to come into your earthly house, which is your soul inside of you, your spirit. People unfairly judged Zacchaeus but Jesus, no matter what you have done, wants to dine with you. On that day, Zacchaeus was saved and his identity crisis was broken. Many of us are like Zacchaeus before his encounter with Christ. God has called us, but we have not had our breakthrough yet because we have not asked for the identity of God through Jesus. We can ask anything through Jesus Christ, and if our request lines up with His will for our lives, it will be ours!

Jesus has the identity of His Father, and that is why we need God's identity in our lives. Couldn't you imagine if we have God's identity through His spiritual DNA how wonderful it would be? The Father helped Jesus on the cross, and now Jesus is trying to help us with a spiritual identity to let our emotions within the soul die to His Spirit. Jesus declared that if you believe you will receive whatever you ask for in prayer (Matthew 21:22). Let me say that again! If we ask anything, He will do it if we believe and obey Him. We need to place ourselves in a position to follow Jesus. If you follow yourself and doubt God, He has a message for you. You are not going to hear from Him right away. Jesus said that those who doubt should think about never receiving what He has for them (John 3:11-12). This means you must stop doubting and start obeying.

Many of us are not getting the spiritual things we want out of life because we have not allowed God to establish our identity in the Lord Jesus Christ. It sounds hard and a crisis is hard, but wouldn't you rather be free than to stay in the situation you are in? That is why we need a relationship. Ask God to show you when you are not obeying instructions from Him, especially when we think our way is the best way. Pray this prayer to God: "Remove any doubt

Lord and help me follow my true identity in You. Because if I follow my true identity in You, the body, soul and spirit will be all together."

In the beginning of John 15, Jesus provides an analogy regarding our relationship with Him using the structure of a vine. He describes Himself as "the true vine" and His Father as "the husbandman." A husbandman's job is to cultivate the plants or crops he is raising. In this analogy, God as the husbandman is caring for the branches, which represent believers. Those who are firmly rooted in the vine of Christ bear fruit, but those who do not, basically believers with superficial faith, are cut off and wither away because they are unproductive. Two of the key points that Jesus makes using this illustration are that "without me ye can do nothing" (John 15:5) and that "if ye abide in me, and my words abide in you, ye shall ask what ye will, and it shall be done unto you" (John 15:7). If we are not rooted in Christ or grafted in as a branch, then we cannot receive the spiritual gifts that we desire and that He wants to give us.

If you are still living in sin or working in ministry within the church and have no understanding of God's Word, I recommend that you follow a ministry that is teaching the identity of Jesus Christ. God wants, as I said before, our body, soul and spirit. He wants all of us. When I face a challenge, Satan says to me, "You know you're a failure. You have faced this before. God is disappointed in you." However, I had to learn the Word, and the Word says that all have sinned and come short of the glory of God. But you are covered through Christ Jesus' blood and you know that Satan is the father of lies. Satan will lie to you because he is trying to steal your identity.

The Bible says in John 10:10 that Satan is a thief! Don't you hate a thief and a liar? You do not want to trust them anymore. So let's wake up and read John 10:10 over again. Satan comes to "STEAL, KILL and DESTROY." If he comes to steal, kill and destroy, there must be something from God's identity that he wants to take away from you. I have news for you. Satan does not love you or this world because he did not create the world or you. God did. God is the One we should be serving, but it seems as if we give more credit to Satan. Satan has an identity with sin and he does it well. He loves nothing that is connected with God.

Satan's influence is manifested through the works of the flesh, which are found in Galatians 5:19-21, and these sinful works will dominate your life when you do not know who you are in Christ. Many of us, even I, have often come to church trying to find relief, and relief is to find our identity in Christ. Some of the crises we have include lack of being loved, trouble finding a meaningful relationship, unhappiness with our status in life, and uncertainty of whether God loves us or not. I noticed that some people in church pretend that they have it altogether and those whom we see outside the church say they have it altogether. But what does it really mean to be altogether? We are covering up and they are covering up. We do not know who is being truthful. Sometimes we are judging them instead of looking within ourselves. Instead of judging, we should show compassion. Compassion is a strong word. Jesus did not tell us to show pity but compassion, and we need to show compassion not just to the world but also to ourselves. Jesus showed compassion on the cross to us, not pity.

This is why we need Christ's identity because He said that He came for us to have life and to have it more abundantly. Yet even with abundant life as new creatures in Christ, we all struggle day by day. Life is a cycle. We can circle around or circle backwards. And an identity crisis can have us in a vicious cycle going backwards. No matter how faith-filled or how responsible you are, you will inevitably find yourself from time to time facing moments that threaten you. For example, some of us have not moved forward in our lives because we are in an identity crisis where we are trying to please people and live up to their expectations. The world judges harshly when we do not measure up to its standards for success and attractiveness. Many people, including those in church, are depressed because they have not reached a desired position in life by a certain age or they feel unworthy of happiness due to negativity that was instilled in them since childhood. They carry enormous burdens that weigh them down, but when we become a child of God, the new creation lifts these burdens and comes with a new identity and description of who we are. The world needs to see this change in us, and the church needs to understand that God requires us to walk in this new creation. You must understand what you must become. When you are asked to identify yourself in the world, you provide an ID such as a driver's license, an employee badge, credit card or debit card. In the world, our identity can be stolen and this brings on fear. Fear of what? Fear of running out of money, losing everything we have worked for, or being wrongly accused of a crime. In the church if we lose our identity in Christ and our branch is cut off, we lose our ministry gifts and will fail in reaching our destiny with God.

Let us get our thoughts together! After reading about the identity crisis that we can have in our lives, where do we go from here? I'm here to tell you that when we lose something from God we can get it back without fearing that it is in someone else's possession. When you lose money, you start asking family and friends if you can borrow from them, oftentimes knowing that you cannot pay it back. God comes in and says that He is our Provider. That is His identity. We should be diligently seeking the promises that God tells us in His Word. We should present ourselves to God, meaning simply to obey Him. Trials and challenges are inevitable. We must learn from them and behind every

challenge we will find God orchestrating the circumstances to build us up. In the following chapters, you will find strategies to help you nurture your identity in Christ, and I pray that those who do not believe may find Christ and His identity. As an old Gospel song says, "It's not my mother, not my father, but it's me O Lord, standing in the need of prayer." We are standing in the need of prayer to walk in His identity.

Chapter Two: Looking in the Mirror

Do you remember Michael Jackson's 1988 hit "Man in the Mirror"? This song resonated with so many people because he was singing about changing the person within and helping those in need. You may have forgotten most of the lyrics, but this song is true because it was about us. At the time of its release, you may not have thought Michael was singing about identity but he was. Most of us are not under the intense public scrutiny he endured as a famous entertainer, but we too face difficult challenges when we strive to change our lives for the better and have more compassion for those less fortunate. If we stop for a moment to think about ourselves, the mirror shows the true reflection. You are all alone looking in the mirror and no one else is around. You do not have to pretend about how you feel or who you really are. Haven't you noticed that sometimes you start talking to the mirror, which is really your conscience talking aloud? You might say, "I thought I had everything in control, but I was really lying to myself" or "Why did I make that decision when I knew better?" Seeing the true reflection of ourselves exposes the personal wounds that we try to cover up, the hurt that we do not want others to see. The mirror allows us to cry when no one else is around to wipe away the tears. Our soul is the inner man that cries, which is our humanness. I explained that God wants our body, soul and spirit. The soul is what we have to correct through the calling and identity of God. Once God has called us, He wants to save us to live by the Holy Spirit. We become that new creature. Old things are

passed away and the new creature has control over our soul (2 Corinthians 5:17).

You can look in the mirror and your soul will show up: feelings, emotions and thoughts. You have thoughts about how you want your day to go or what position you would like to be in several years from now. This is why we need the love of God in our lives, so when we look in that mirror we see a true identity of God's Spirit in us instead of our soul's spirit.

For you and me, we must start enjoying our lives by having
the true identity of God. So when we do have to face that
mirror, we see that true DNA of Christ. As He is, so are we.
It is God's mirror (the Bible) that reflects you. The mirror
that God gives you is 1 John 4:17, explaining that "because
as he is, so are we in this world."

One of the hardest things I had to do was to look in the
mirror and hear my emotions pour out through my prayers
from the inner man, which is related to my soul, mind and
heart. God promises to strengthen us with power through
His Spirit in our inner man when we pray, but I struggled
with this in church leadership, especially with people going
in and out of church. I also had difficult challenges in the
places where I worked for over 20 years. My inner man,
full of my emotions, would say to me, "But you have God,
the Holy Spirit and Jesus! How could you struggle with
anything?" Well, my soul had not completely died all the
way to God's Spirit or my emotions. So when people hurt
me or said things about me that were not true, my emotions
influenced me to dislike them. I knew disliking people was
wrong, but to me and in my soul it felt good. I declared that
I did not want to be bothered with them anymore, and I
asked God to keep them away from me. Had I forgiven

them? At that time I had not, and I wept and cried out to God, asking, "Why me, Lord? What have I done to deserve this?" Why were close friends whom I had constantly prayed for and even given money to out of my own pocket being so spiteful and vindictive? Many times I sacrificed and let things go financially in my own house to see that others got what they needed. Why was I being treated this way? Looking back on the distress of these experiences, I realized that I made the decision to assist some people on my own without asking God whom He wanted me to help. Have you ever questioned yourself in your mind that God would be proud of you if you helped someone? Obviously, you want to be blessed by Him when you do what we consider "good deeds." We are thinking about our good deeds and being rewarded in heaven one day when we go back with Him. However, my mistake was that I did not wait for God to tell me to help specific people. If I had, I would have been spared a lot of disappointment. This is another example of where I have learned that the identity of God must come in. I should have prayed and asked God what I should have done instead of operating in the sensitivity of my flesh, but He had mercy on me when I cried out to Him about my pain.

God answered my cry by showing me what genuine love is in His identity. I had to learn the true meaning of what Jesus said in Matthew 5:44: "Love your enemies, bless them that curse you, do good to them that hate you, and pray for them which despitefully use you, and persecute you." Continuing to pray for those who used and persecuted me in ministry was not easy by any means. We often say in church that "God knows my heart." Well, He certainly does, and you definitely cannot fake your way through praying for people who betrayed you. God knows if you are being sincere or not. By yielding myself in prayer before Him, I also had to look within my identity that God had given me by the fruit of His Spirit. In Galatians 5:22, love is the first fruit listed of the Spirit. As a reference to John 15, love is the first fruit that should be growing on our branch as we are connected to the vine, who is Jesus. After love comes joy, peace, longsuffering, gentleness, goodness, faith, meekness, and temperance. God showed me that if I did not have love I would not produce the other fruit that follows. If I allowed my anger in my flesh to manifest because of how my enemies and those who I thought were friends treated me, I would be withered as a branch. I had to learn to forgive those who hurt me and forgive myself for not listening to God, and I began to take heed to Isaiah 26:3, which tells us that if our mind is stayed on God that He will keep us in perfect peace. One of the most powerful revelations of love that I found as a servant of God is Jesus' response to His disciple Peter in John 21:15-18. This was Jesus' third appearance to His disciples after His resurrection, and after dining with them by the sea of Tiberias, Jesus ministered to the hurt of Peter in a special way. Peter had denied Christ three times before the Lord was put on trial to be crucified, but Peter's denial was the result of fear and not betrayal like Judas. Jesus asked Peter if he loved Him three times, and by the third time the Word of God says that Peter was "grieved" and Jesus told him, "Feed my sheep" (John 21:17). The *Life Application Study Bible* provides this commentary regarding Peter's repentance: "Peter's life changed when he finally realized who Jesus was. His occupation changed from fisherman to evangelist; his identity changed from impetuous to 'rock'" (1592). Similar to Peter, my identity changed to know that the love of God in me and His calling on my life required me to "feed His sheep." No matter the obstacles I faced while leading my church, God's love would help me to overcome. I have given you the example of Peter, and you can also compare what we see in the mirror to the classic fairytale of Snow White. We all know that when Snow White's evil stepmother looked into the mirror she expected it to tell her that she was the "fairest in the land." Although she had an evil heart, she was the fairest in her kingdom for a specific time. The mirror confirmed this. However, when Snow White came of age her beauty was matchless. When the mirror told the evil stepmother that she was no longer the most beautiful, the wickedness that was in her heart fully manifested. The mirror will reflect the truth about your soul if you stare into it long enough.

The Bible also provides an analogy of a mirror in 1 Corinthians 13:12, where the Apostle Paul wrote, "For now we see through a glass, darkly; but then face to face: now I know in part; but then shall I know even as also I am known." "Darkly" can be described as a distorted image that clouds our view or understanding. This can result from the confusion that our soul often brings, but when we come "face to face" with Christ we will see things clearly through the Holy Spirit. Then we can look into the mirror and say that we have the identity of the Lord.

Chapter Three: Know your Identity

As you read this chapter, I want you to learn who you are in Christ. We are living in distressing times, so this chapter is very important. Why? Because we have become confused and frustrated. Confusion and frustration are everyday challenges in the world and in the church. From our childhood to our adulthood, we still have people labeling us as failures. At birth, our outlook on life is shaped by our family regarding whether we will be successful or not. However, in God's eyes He loves us for who we are. He created us to follow Him and to get to know Him and receive His gift of the Holy Spirit. We do not understand how to follow Him if we have not had the

Word of God taught to us as we study the Bible. Here are some strategies that can help you know your identity in Christ.

1. **Read your Word (the Bible)**. Reading your Word is essential in knowing your spiritual identity. Once you begin to consistently read Scripture, then study your Word because you are going to need it on this journey in life. In 2 Timothy 2:15, we are told to study to show ourselves "approved unto God" so that we can rightly divide "the word of truth." Rightly dividing the Word means that we will know how to apply scriptural principles to our lives. God's Word will not be effective if you do not apply it daily, and the consequence of lack of study is not knowing God's true purpose for your life. Think of it this way. A person who wants to be a doctor or a lawyer has to study to become excellent in these professions. He or she must apply to medical school and law school respectively. The medical student will learn about the human body and specialize in a specific field of medicine, and the law student will choose an area of practice. When medical students become doctors, they must apply what they learned in school to successfully treat patients, and when law students become lawyers, they must master the precepts of legal strategy to argue a case in court. The same

applies to God's Word. You must study it so that you can operate in its power as a believer.

2. **Pray without ceasing (1 Thessalonians 5:17).** This means every day, anywhere and at any time. One of the best known prayer warriors in the Bible was Daniel. Daniel held a senior administrative position in the Babylonian government, a kingdom in ancient Mesopotamia. Much like our present times, Babylon had all of the troubles that we see globally: natural disasters, corrupt politicians and assassinations. During all of this, the Bible informs us that Daniel diligently prayed three times a day (Daniel 6:10). His colleagues became jealous of his devotion to his faith in God, which granted him distinctive favor with King Darius. Therefore, Daniel's colleagues devised an evil plan and drafted a law for the king to sign that banned prayer to God, landing Daniel in a lion's den. The Bible tells of the miracle of God shutting up the mouths of the lions (Daniel 6:22). Daniel's prayers delivered him. Today, your lion's den may be a job, your family, your health, or a financial crisis. Prayer will get you through! Philippians 4:6 tells us to be "careful for nothing" but by "prayer and supplication with thanksgiving" to let our "requests be made known unto God." Keep prayer on your mind and on your lips, and you will see changes in your life.

3. **Go to a Bible-based church.** Going to a Bible-based church helps because the Word tells us not to forsake the

assembling of ourselves (Hebrews 10:25) and that faith comes by hearing (Romans 10:17). Church is a sacred place where the people of God are strengthened and built up in His Word. We find solace in God's promises, rest in peace during despair, and receive encouragement to carry out the divine calling on our lives. Fellowshipping with believers provides us with a strong community of faith.

4. **Be obedient to God.** Being obedient is to listen to God's voice and to follow the Word, which is your Bible. Start trusting in the Word. Obedience means a lot to God because when we wholeheartedly submit ourselves to His statutes we establish a covenant relationship with Him. Obedience to God is not about keeping rules and regulations in a dull, religious routine. It is about communion with Him, which cleanses the soul and brings it under subjection to the Holy Spirit. This is why God said in Jeremiah 31:33 that "this is the covenant I will make with the people of Israel after that time ... I will put my law in their minds (our souls) and write it on their hearts. I will be their God, and they will be my people" (New International Version).

5. **Ask God for wisdom and knowledge.** God is the only one who can give you insight about your spiritual life and life in general. James 1:5 tells us that if we "lack wisdom"

we need to ask God who gives "to all *men* liberally, and upbraideth not." "Upbraideth" in the Greek translation here means that God will not "taunt" or "chide" us for asking. He desires for us to seek His counsel in everything that we do.

6. **Finally, change.** When you change something, your behavior and attitude are transformed. You change the way you think, the way you act, and how you use the power within you. Once God's power changes you, Ephesians 5:18 says you become filled with the Spirit and that is the change you will have – God's Spirit!

After reading these strategies, you can see we need the heart of God to allow Him to help us control the wrong identity of our soul and use the new identity along with the Holy Spirit. Remember, as you get more of God in you, the greater you become. Now, let's really make this personal! Say this to yourself, "As I get more of God in me, the greater I will become!" You just made Satan mad! Don't you feel good about that? Satan hates the fact that you now know the truth that he is defeated when the identity of God in you is above the identity of your soul.

The Bible says that we must be "sober" and "vigilant" because our "adversary the devil" walks about as a "roaring lion seeking whom he may devour" (1 Peter 5:8). So when we use our own human ability, which is our soul, we set ourselves up to be consumed by the devil, who was kicked out of heaven because he lost his true identity in God through rebellion. If we are consumed by our enemy, we too can miss God's blessings and miss our divine purpose, especially His anointing.

We become sober and vigilant by losing our own identity within our soul. When we use our own identity, it leads to pain and disappointment. That is why we need a shepherd to guide us, and you will find in Psalm 23 that God is a true Shepherd! In addition to Psalm 23, one of the Scriptures that helped me is Psalm 37:4. I started to "delight myself in the Lord" and in His Word and walk in His ways. I lost the identity of my soul and God blessed me with a new identity. Do not forget John 8:44, which states that the enemy is the father of lies. Satan will lie about God and he will also lie about you. You must know the truth about your identity in Christ. He will never leave you, nor forsake you (Hebrews 13:5). Listen to His voice. I found out there is never a time God is not talking. There is no choir so loud that the voice of God cannot be heard if we listen. I am convinced the problem is sometimes spiritual laziness rather than ignorance. When we feel weak and powerless, we must break loose from those things that are hindering us from following God's identity. Read Philippians 4:13. Say it aloud, "I can do ALL THINGS through Christ who strengthens me!" Keep repeating it until you feel it! Meditate on it.

Chapter Four: We are more than a Conqueror

(Check your DNA)

P eople often marvel at the fact that God, an omnipotent, omnipresent Spirit, actually has a Son in Jesus. The Bible records Jesus' miraculous conception in Matthew 1:18, telling us, "When as his mother Mary was espoused to Joseph, before they came together, she was found with child of the Holy Ghost." In verse 20, the angel of the Lord appears to Joseph to reassure him that Mary has not stepped out of their union and sinned: "… for that which is conceived in her is of the Holy Ghost." Now as we know there were no DNA tests during biblical times,

and a child's identity was traced through his or her father's bloodline. With Joseph being Jesus' earthly father, Jesus was tied to the lineage of King David, but Jesus also had

David's biological lineage through His mother Mary, which includes the 42 generations that Jesus came through. In natural conception, we know that blood develops in the ovum after the male sperm fertilizes it. Perhaps the most fascinating thing about Jesus' conception is that He received His blood from the Father! This is the blood we need spiritually in our DNA. The bloodline of Jesus is powerful! Many hymns such as "O the blood of Jesus" and "At the Cross," along with Scripture, testify to this. Jesus' blood purifies us from sin, heals us, and brings us into covenant relationship with God. We are able to have a relationship with God because the blood of Jesus sanctifies our souls. In the Old Testament, the blood of bulls and goats was offered on an altar to "make atonement for the soul" (Leviticus 17:11); however, the priests had to

annually perform these sacrifices for the people because there was "a remembrance again *made* of sins every year" (Hebrews 10:3). Jesus made atonement for our souls on the cross – a sacrifice that remains forever – so when you receive Christ as your personal Savior you become a living sacrifice through His blood. Jesus' blood purged us from all of our sins and is now concealed within our souls, which is the everlasting atonement. Through Him, we can conquer anything! The blood works with the Holy Spirit, Jesus, and God the Father to have us to live the way the Word wants us to live. It is important to remember that the blood does not keep us from sinning. What keeps us from sinning is the lifestyle of the Holy Spirit.

Being more than a conqueror in Christ means we have victory over any situation that we go through, as stated in Romans 8:37. This is a powerful Scripture! It tells us that by being God's people the Conqueror is in us, and what He has conquered we can conquer. No matter what it looks

like, it's already done! This is why we need a relationship with God. When the Spirit of God's DNA comes through us, it not only helps us to go through things, but it brings us into a relationship. We can ask God for anything and we do not have to beg.

You probably have never thought about DNA in the Spirit, but consider your earthly DNA. Doctors ask us questions about our family history when we go in for our annual checkups. We fill out forms about the diseases that run in our family to provide the doctor with background history. This helps the doctor practice preventive medicine in hopes of keeping us healthy so that we do not become susceptible to the illnesses that may be in our bloodline. This is the same way with our spiritual bloodline. Jesus will take away our sins from the old man and give us the spiritual, preventive medicine that we need in Him, which transforms us into the new man. We were born in sin and shaped in iniquity, but when we get Jesus' DNA through the Father

and follow the identity of Christ, the nature of the old man will cease by having the Holy Spirit. The Holy Spirit will guide you, teach you, and talk with you daily when you allow the true identity of Jesus to be in your life. CONQUER. CONQUER. CONQUER. We must conquer the old man! We must conquer what people have said about us. For example, a family member or friend may say that you are going to be just like your mother or father, but your parents may be mean or may not like to be around others. As a new creature, you do not have to follow the pattern of your parents' personalities because you will have the Holy Spirit. Christ died for this new man.

Jesus knows that everything is not going to be perfect in our holy lifestyle, so He commands that we follow Him, the perfect man. If we allow ourselves to trust in Jesus Christ and not walk after the flesh, I guarantee our lives will be better. I guarantee it because my life is better due to following the identity of Jesus Christ every day.

Sometimes it is a hard task. This is why we have to stand on the promises of God and study and learn them for ourselves through these troubled times. I always read about David, the man after God's own heart, and his writing in the book of Psalms. Crying out to the Lord, David states that God will hear us, so I pattern my life after his example. I cry out to the Lord as much as I can, asking Him to help me know and walk in His identity. Praise God! He heard my cry!

Chapter Five: Lord help my Unbelief in trusting the True Identity

To reach your spiritual identity you need to have God help you with doubt. Doubts will come when we choose to follow Jesus' identity. Sometimes doubt will settle in when we do not read God's Word and ask for understanding of what we have read. Jesus Christ operated through the identity of His Father. He never doubted God because of what He knew He had to do and that was to die for the whole world that we might be saved. Many people that I have come across and have kept conversation with knew nothing about the identity of God and Jesus Christ, God's Son. Some told me that they never heard about

Christ's identity or having a relationship with Him. They only knew what they heard in church – that God loved them and that they were going to heaven. They were instructed to give God their hearts and to do the best they could. When I was a child people were constantly told, "Come to church, come to church!" People mistook the word church for just being a building because that is all they grew up knowing. But really, the church is in you. When Jesus called us to Him, He specifically said, "I am the church." In Matthew 16:18, Jesus said to Peter, "Upon this rock I will build my church; and the gates of hell shall not prevail against it." We need to know that Christ is the church, and we worship Him in a building. The Greek word for church is "ekklesia," which means "a calling out." This is referring to bodies of believers where Jesus Christ is the Head.

In the beginning of 1 Corinthians 14:23, the Apostle Paul writes about the whole church coming "together into one place." Believers who come to church make up the body of Christ. In Matthew 18:20, Jesus also said that when two or three are gathered in His name, He is in the midst of them. Those who are in the midst of Christ are the ones who are saved, the ones who overcome doubt and the ones who know how to pray. God will add people to the church who have been called out, those who are believers. So many people make the mistake of "going to church" on Sundays to see what the "physical building" has on the inside instead of bringing the church within them. When we come to a building and our church is not right within us, we are in trouble. This prevents us from receiving the spiritual breakthrough, refreshing and deliverance that God has for us. We use Matthew 16:18 to explain "our church." You are God's church! And wherever the church is, Christ should be there because you bring Him in. With Christ within you as your church, you have His identity and you have the power to overcome anything that the world attempts to bring against you (1 John 4:4).

Colossians 1:18 states very clearly that Jesus is "the head of the body," the church in you, "who is the beginning, the firstborn from the dead." Doubt sets in when we do not know the meaning of a church. The church was purchased by Christ's blood (Acts 20:28). God is not coming for a building. He is coming for the church within you. I wanted to explain this because we get God's identity through Christ's blood. If you are called out, you will not say that you do not want to go to church because your church is willing to receive prayer and the Word. Your church is eager for instruction on how to seek God, how to walk like

God, and how to be true identity Christians. I used to ask myself if the church is following Christ why are there so many churches with different teachings? This will bring doubt into anybody's mind, and we start believing in other things except Christ. We start trusting the leadership instead of God, and when we just trust the leadership and do not follow the church in us, which is our Head, Jesus Christ, we tend to have doubt. The church is a celebration of believing the same thing. This is why I want God to help us not to doubt because when doubt settles in that is when difficulty comes. We ask ourselves, "Does it matter what we believe?" This is a doubt question. We ask, "Why do I have to go to church" and we point fingers when the pastor, bishop, or overseer makes a mistake. Then we say, "I can serve God at home," but the Bible tells us not to forsake "the assembling of ourselves together" (Hebrews 10:25). When you become a doubter, you forget to look at yourself. Remember, chapter two tells you to look in the mirror. Trusting God's identity is so real. I am not just thinking about you, but I am also thinking about myself. I was once tied up in myself, and it looked like God was doing everything for everyone else except me. I got angry. I was doing what I thought was right, but as I said regarding looking in the mirror, instead of listening to others telling me what was right and what was wrong I began to see my true identity through the mirror. That is when I found out that God is real from studying the Word and believing who He is. He is real, and the Holy Ghost is real as the Bible says. You will find the true identity of God through the Word. Trust in Him.

In order to change we must be, as the late civil rights activist Fannie Lou Hamer famously said, "Sick and tired of being sick and tired." Transform your life to go God's way because what is missing is the path you are taking to God's identity. We are not able to change the world solely with our own ideas, but I know my life can be better if I choose Jesus Christ as my personal Savior. Have you ever been at a point in your life where you doubt everything and it is so hard for you to believe or trust something that you cannot see? It is a horrible feeling because we start believing everything in our past instead of believing in the

future. Our future is Christ. There are times when we are going to have difficulty in understanding the ways of God, but if we trust in Him, the challenge of knowing Him will be rewarded. Have you ever studied the biblical meaning of the word trust? Trust means you believe what God has done for you and has given you. He has given you that new man, or as the Word says, the new creature that is in you. I am sharing this with you because it has helped me not doubt but trust in the wonderful Savior, Jesus Christ. By doubting, your lifestyle changes in a negative way. You find yourself not wanting to be around church people because you begin to believe that they are phony. And nothing they say has come true for you. But it's not about them. It's about God and you. You know the soul that I have been talking about? It talks back strongly. It wants you and me to trust it and not the Holy Spirit.

One of the most well-known Christian hymns in the church is "Trust and Obey." The chorus says, "Trust and obey, for there's no other way; to be happy in Jesus, but to trust and obey." The Scripture says in Psalm 146:5 that "happy *is he* that *hath* the God of Jacob for his help, whose hope *is* in the LORD his God." The Hebrew translation of "happy" is one who is "blessed." You are blessed when you put your trust in God, not people, because He is the One who sustains you.

It is difficult for many people in church to trust in God today because they feel that others have hurt them. This is why we have so much unbelief. Some of us have said preachers or the church want too much money, and we have complained that church service is too long. However, in your old identity you did not care how long a party was, or a movie, or a concert. You did not complain about these activities, and you paid money to participate in them.

When we follow Jesus' identity, we should have even more zeal for Him. This is our true way of life, and this means we cannot doubt Him but we must trust Him. I found out the hard way that trusting in people would not work. Trusting myself definitely does not work, but belief in Jesus Christ will work every time. When you have the spiritual DNA of Jesus Christ, it will help you not to trust in man but to believe that God's Word and the Holy Spirit are true. Then you will begin to say, "Oh, how I love Jesus! Because He first loved me!"

Chapter Six: Teaching and Preaching

When you closely study the life of Jesus Christ in the New Testament, you will learn that He did not do a lot of preaching, and by preaching, I mean the traditional format of sermons many of us heard growing up in church. Jesus was a master teacher and when He did preach, as He did with His "Sermon on the Mount" recorded in the fifth chapter of Matthew, the Scripture says that "he opened his mouth, and taught them" (Matthew 5:2). The Sermon on the Mount contained the Beatitudes, which are nine blessings that Jesus used to explain the Godly character of believers. We get the word beatitude from the Latin "beatus," which means "happy" or "fortunate." Jesus begins each Beatitude by proclaiming, "Blessed are," and after stating these declarations Jesus then focuses on some of the primary principles of the kingdom of God. Since the Beatitudes are declarations, you have to study the teaching behind them so that you fully understand what Jesus was saying. For example, in the first Beatitude Jesus says, "Blessed *are* the poor in spirit: for theirs is the kingdom of heaven." "Poor in spirit" here is referring to someone with a humble attitude, a person who is not arrogant or proud. Jesus was explaining that a humble person is blessed.

The Bible says that when Jesus began teaching people were "astonished" at His doctrine because His words were powerful (Luke 4:32). One of the reasons for this was that back in Jesus' time so many people were used to ceremonial rituals when worshipping God. The religious leaders – the Pharisees and the Sadducees – were especially guilty of this because they were full of pride in their outward showing of their religion. When Jesus began teaching about having a personal relationship with God, the religious leaders rejected Him due to their stubbornness in wanting to cling to their traditions. The teachings of Jesus that had people "astonished" were His parables. A parable is a short story that has a spiritual lesson. Let's take a look at two of them: the Parable of the Sower and the Parable of the Prodigal Son.

The Parable of the Sower is found in Matthew 13:1-23, Mark 4:1-20 and Luke 8:4-15. Jesus begins this story by speaking to multitudes and saying that a sower went forth to sow seeds. While sowing these seeds, some fell by the wayside and birds came and devoured them. Some seeds fell on "stony places" and grew up fast, but because they were not rooted in the earth, they withered away from the heat of the sun. Some seeds fell among thorns and grew up but were choked, but the remaining seed fell on good

ground and produced fruit, some an hundredfold, some sixtyfold, and some thirtyfold. Jesus explained this parable to His disciples that the sower is sowing the Word of God, which is the seed. The seed falling by the wayside represents people who hear the Word, but Satan comes and steals what has been sown in their hearts. The seeds that fall on the stony ground represent people who immediately receive the Word with joy, but they lack root, meaning that they do not nourish their faith. They endure for a while, but when they are persecuted or attacked for their belief in Christ they become offended. The seeds that fall among thorns refer to people who hear the Word, but they are drawn away and enticed by the temptations and cares of the world. They "choke" and become unfruitful. However, the seeds that fall on good ground are the people who hear the Word and produce fruit in their walk of faith with God. As mentioned in chapter two, the fruit of the Spirit is found in Galatians 5:22 and begins with love. As you go back and study this parable, focus on Jesus' emphasis regarding the seed of the Word in your life. The seed of the Word is essential to your identity in Christ. Do not let it fall by the wayside. Work on nurturing your seed (reading and studying the Word) so that you will be strong in your faith and produce fruit.

The Parable of the Prodigal Son is a story that has brought comfort to so many due to Jesus' illustration of the unconditional love of God as our heavenly Father. In this parable found in Luke 15:11-32, Jesus tells the story of a young man who is eager to get out into the world on his own, and he asks his father, a wealthy man, for all of his inheritance – his "portion of goods" – so that he can leave home. This young man has an older brother and their father divides his estate at the request of his younger son. The younger son, like many young people who are restless today, goes out and lives a "riotous" life in a "far country." He parties hard and wastes all of his inheritance on frivolous pleasures. A famine soon comes upon the land

and this young man ends up broke. He finds a lowly job feeding pigs and is destitute and hungry. None of the fast friends he partied with offered him any money. After suffering for a while, the young man begins to reflect on his father's household and realizes that the servants were cared for and ate well. The young man "came to himself" before he returned home. This is really showing the identity that he had of his father because he came to understand what his father stood for. He confessed his transgressions to his father and said that he would take the role of a servant because he no longer felt worthy to be called a son. The father was overwhelmed with joy to see him, and I could imagine that he was glad his son came back home alive. The young man looked bad and had the stench of the pigs on him, but his father did not care about this. The father tells his servants to bring forth "the best robe" and put it on his son, and to kill "the fatted calf" so that everyone could celebrate his son's safe return. The father represents the identity of God as our Father for us. The young man represents the new creature for whom Jesus died. When the young man confessed his wrongdoing to his father, his father had already forgiven him. Jesus is bringing the best by giving us the Holy Spirit when we confess our sins to Him and not man.

Many of you reading this book may have been a prodigal son or daughter. Perhaps you left the church and walked out into the world looking to find fulfillment for the void in your heart. Some of you may have sinned, but your heavenly Father, just like the father of the prodigal son, is waiting with open arms for you to return. The prodigal son did not lose his identity as "his father's son" when he returned home; rather, he was restored to his rightful place in his family. God will do the same for you. If you have left Him, come home. He will celebrate and restore you.

Another spiritual lesson that Jesus brought forth in this parable is the attitude of the older brother. Like many people who have been in church all of their lives, the older brother served his father and did not disobey his commandments, but one essential attribute was missing: love. The older brother served his father not with joyfulness of heart but with complacency. As the firstborn, he felt entitled. When the younger brother returned home, his older brother's heart was hardened so much that he refused to take part in the celebration. Yet, the father also had compassion for his elder son. "Son," his father said, "thou art ever with me, and all that I have is thine" (Luke 15:31). When you are serving God faithfully with true love for Him in your heart, everything that He has belongs to you. You do not have to worry about losing what God has planned to give you in your life. Your inheritance is set. Serve God with joy and love your brothers and sisters. Do not worry about who loves you in the church or in the world. The Parable of the Prodigal Son shows us that God loves us very much because His identity is love. When you love, you will not have time to find fault in others or judge them. It is not up to us to judge but for God to judge because He knows everything about us.

Many times I have noticed some of my friends who are ministers do more preaching than teaching. They say preaching fires them up. I believe that if you are going to preach more there should also be a time to teach the Word of God. Being an overseer over my ministry, I used to preach all the time, but now the Lord has me teaching more of the Word, even on Sundays, so that the people will have a better understanding and gain wisdom and knowledge. The reason I teach sometimes on Sundays is because I noticed the people enjoy the Word of God in a less formal setting. In addition, it allows the flock to study the Word more for themselves. Preaching aims at the heart. It is fiery and oftentimes very exciting to the congregation.

Teaching is the information of the Gospel. It explains the Gospel so you can understand it. The Bible does not really separate teaching and preaching. Preaching announces the good news and teaching explains the clarification, application and exhortation of the Word to those already informed, as well as those who are just beginning to learn the Scriptures.

By studying, I found out that the writers of the first three New Testament books are known as the synoptic Gospel authors due to writing to specific audiences. Matthew was written to the Jews, Mark was written to the Romans, and Luke was written to the Greeks. Matthew thought of Jesus more as a teacher, while Mark and Luke record a lot of Jesus' preaching. One of the unique ways the Holy Spirit used these men in recording their Gospel accounts is that their distinctive personalities are reflected in their writing. Matthew was a tax collector, so he paid close attention to Jesus' teachings about money and giving to the poor while also documenting what Jesus taught about significant life topics, such as worry, lust, anger, and forgiveness. Mark, also known as John Mark, was not one of the 12 disciples. Since his primary audience was Rome, you will find Mark recording many miracles in addition to Jesus' teachings.

The Romans, with their admiration for logic and reason, liked to see tangible results. Mark records more miracles than any other Gospel. Luke was a Greek physician, and in writing his Gospel to his own people, you will find that he used poetry and songs of praise as a way to make a cultural connection with them.

When you begin to study the synoptic Gospel accounts of Jesus, you will notice that when He preached much of His emphasis was on the kingdom of God. When Jesus taught, He was giving the people spiritual principles and instruction on how to apply their faith in their daily walk with God. Teaching gets you to study the Word because the pastor can slow it down, just as Jesus did in His settings with His disciples and the multitudes who came to hear Him. This is why I mentioned that we need to be taught more, even to find out about the true identity of God in our lives. If you are already a believer, I hope you understand that it is time to share the good news about Jesus Christ in your life with others, and if you do not know your identity through Christ, it is time to hear from not just the preacher or teacher but mainly from God. Remember the Scripture in Matthew 6:33: "But seek ye first the kingdom of God, and his righteousness; and all these things shall be added unto you." To those who have never attended church or go to church, but have not given their lives to Christ, you need to seek God for your true identity as well.

Chapter Seven: Staying in the Word
(God is the Word)

God is good and His Word is excellent! I talked a lot about myself in this book and how I have been changed by the consistent studying and reading of God's Word. Having operated in the office of a pastor for many years and now moving into leadership as an overseer, which the Lord called me to, I initially did not understand why He changed my position. I felt more comfortable being a pastor. Many pastors know how to "preach people happy," but God had me not to preach people happy but to teach them right from wrong, especially in this day. He told me about my identity in Christ, and I began focusing on the identity of Christ in Bible study so the people in my flock would know who they are in God. One of the things I noticed is that it is a struggle to get to the spiritual level of what the Word says about us. We must read the promises of God to see if we believe what He says. You will not know God's promises until you get into His Word because this will keep you near Him.

How many times have you heard 1 Peter 2:9 quoted in church? You probably memorized it if you grew up attending Sunday school as a child. It says, "But ye *are* a chosen generation, a royal priesthood, an holy nation, a peculiar people; that ye should shew forth the praises of him who hath called you out of darkness into his marvelous light."

Anyone who is familiar with the Old Testament knows how significant generations were due to people being identified through their family bloodlines. God is often referred to as "the God of Abraham, Isaac and Jacob," three generations

of men whose seed would establish the nation of Israel during the dispensation of the law. Wouldn't it be wonderful if God called us to do what they did in following His identity? Now when we come over to the dispensation of grace established under Christ, Peter calls us "a chosen generation." Let me repeat that, a chosen generation! It is a powerful thing to be chosen by God! Peter is able to make this declaration because we have been made "nigh" or near to God through the blood of Christ (Ephesians 2:13). Therefore, not only are we chosen but we are royalty as well as "peculiar." Peculiar in the Greek translation here means "purchased possession," again indicating that we belong to God through Christ's sacrifice on the cross. Now that we belong to God, we have a royal identity, and with royalty comes authority and dominion. What do we have authority over? All the power of the enemy (Satan), spiritual wickedness in high places, and any entity of sin. Sin no longer has the power to enslave us in depression, sickness, hopelessness, poverty, frustration, hatred, and despair, but do we exercise this authority as part of our daily lifestyle in the Spirit? The spiritual struggle is real because we often do not use what God has given us and resort to fighting by what we see in the flesh. In the world, there is an old adage of admonishing one not to bring a knife to a gunfight. A similar concept applies in the spiritual realm. You cannot fight in spiritual warfare with armor designed for physical combat. Everlast boxing gloves are useless for someone shackled and tormented with a spirit of anxiety. With the identity that we have in Christ and the authority He has given us, we have the means to stand boldly against the wiles and weaponry of the devil (Ephesians 6:11). It is our generational right!

Another well-known Bible promise is Colossians 2:10. In this verse, the Apostle Paul wrote that "ye are complete in him (Christ), which is the head of all principality and power." Here again, we are seeing our identity in Christ through His spiritual jurisdiction. Being "complete" in Christ means that we are mature in Him and follow what the Word has said. When we cross-reference this promise with Ephesians 3:17-20, we find that when Christ dwells in our hearts by faith that we are "rooted and grounded in love." Paul goes on to explain that this foundation of love passes the knowledge of the world and enables us to be "filled with all the fullness of God." Having the fullness of God takes us well beyond the surface belief in His existence. Yes, it is good to believe in God, but if you just settle for surface belief, you will never know your true identity in Him. You will never be "complete" and your faith will lack maturity, which will put you in a position of spiritual vulnerability when you face critical obstacles in your life. When you are complete in Christ, however, you lack nothing, and you can go with boldness to God for whatever you need (Hebrews 4:16). Being "perfect" or "mature" means following the perfect man, who is Jesus Christ (Ephesians 4:13). We often do not follow the principles of the "perfect man." It seems to be so easy for us to follow the instructions for other things that we pursue. Take school, for example. When you are studying for a college degree, you follow the instructions of your professor. You strive to get an "A" on every test or essay assignment because an "A" is evaluated as excellent. If you want to do well in your classes, you will not be lazy and settle for lower grades when you have the talent and potential to do better. God wants us to apply this same zeal when reading the Bible. We must study to show ourselves "approved unto God," meaning we must take time in the Scriptures to get to know God so that we can "rightly divide the Word" (2 Timothy 2:15). Being able to rightly divide the Word means that you have no questions or confusion about who you are in Christ. You are confident in His promises and you obtain wisdom and knowledge from your study in how to apply the Word in every area of your life.

One of the most precious promises that we find in knowing God is having peace. Isaiah 26:3-4 says, "Thou wilt keep *him* in perfect peace, *whose* mind *is* stayed *on thee*: because he trusteth in thee. Trust ye in the LORD for ever: for in the LORD JEHOVAH *is* everlasting strength." Peace from God comes from trusting Him, and trust is the Old

Testament word for faith. Our identity in Christ is built on trusting God. You will not trust someone you do not know. God is our Creator. He is our Way Maker, our Provider, and most of all, He is everything we need. He has no shortcomings. It is hard to lean on God because He is a Spirit and we are seeing things with the fleshly eye, and this is where we have lost our identity. But trust me, once you get the hang of believing and trusting God, you will find out there is nobody like the Lord. Go to God and tell Him what your problems are and do not try to figure them out. Proverbs 3:5 tells us not to lean to our own understanding, but in all our ways to acknowledge God and He will direct our path. So study the Word to show yourself approved unto God, so you will not have to lean to your own understanding but believe in the One who is guiding you, who is the wonderful, precious Jesus Christ. The Bible says that the Word is sharper than a two-edged sword (Hebrews 4:12). It can cut you. Reading the Scriptures and meditating on them will make you a saved and sanctified person, and you will be able to follow the DNA and identity of Christ. Once you find that your identity is like His identity, you can help others to receive what you have. We must work on this. We must strive to discipline ourselves in the Word to become better followers of Christ.

Start weighing it out and looking in that mirror. Read, study, and hear the Word of God, so you will find what is stopping you from following Jesus' identity. Have you ever been in a position where you had power over something in the flesh? You feel like you have accomplished something and everyone is now listening to you. You feel that you have improved your life but sometimes that power can get you into trouble, and you are no longer a listener but a dictator. If you say you have God, I want you to check and see if you are following God's identity with the power He has given you. If you have not received His power, you will find out your human power is so different from His power, and the devil really enjoys it when you use your power instead of God's power. Do not forget that Satan only has the power to do harm to us when we allow him, but for those who do not have the true power of God, Satan will trample over them because he hates everything that God has created. He not only hates those who know Christ, but also those who have not had a chance to know Him. For those who know Christ, go after His true identity, and for those who want to be in Christ, call on Him to receive the greatness of His identity. My heart's desire is for you to get to know Him! As you have noticed, I am not just talking to Christians, but to everyone God is calling.

Superhero Sidebar

When thinking about my destiny and identity with God, sometimes I like to compare this to the superheroes that many of us idolized as children from watching movies and reading comic books. I loved Superman as a child because of his strength and his power, and of course he was handsome. Wonder Woman served as a feminine force of grace and beauty, and I later became a fan of Spider-Man for his youthful humor and his ability to discern danger using his "spidey sense." Besides their extraordinary physical gifts, these heroes have another significant characteristic in common: their super names are their aliases that they use to fight crime and evil. They are known by their civilian identities in their daily interactions with people. Superman is Clark Kent, the name his adoptive parents gave him, and he works as a reporter for *The Daily Planet* in the fictional city of Metropolis. Wonder Woman is Diana Prince, who in some comic versions works in military intelligence, and Spider-Man is Peter Parker, a teenager dealing with adolescent struggles at home and in school.

I am sure that many of us pretended to be one of these or another superhero while growing up. We wanted to fly like Superman, kick butt in hand-to-hand combat like Wonder Woman, and leap from buildings like Spider-Man. Some of us dressed up like them for Halloween. A fun as well as powerful reflection for me now regarding these heroes is that God, through His identity in Jesus Christ, has given us greater dominant and authoritative power. Superman has X-ray vision. God has given us the ability to walk by faith so that we are not burdened by what we see in the natural (2 Corinthians 5:7). Wonder Woman fights with a sword

and shield. God has given us these in our spiritual armor: our "sword of the Spirit" is His Word (Ephesians 6:17) and our "shield of faith" enables us "to quench all the fiery darts of the wicked" (Ephesians 6:16). The spiritual equivalent of Spider-Man's "spidey sense" is discernment. In 1 Kings 3:9, King Solomon asked God for "an understanding heart" so that he could "discern between good and bad."

The best part about the spiritual power that God has given us is that we do not have to conceal ourselves in our daily lives like our beloved superheroes! We do not need aliases or secondary names! God wants to expose us for His glory in the world. People need to see the power of God being manifested in their lives. They need to witness miraculous healing and deliverance. As Jesus was preparing to return to heaven after He was raised from the dead, He told His disciples that they would do "greater works" (John 14:12), which means that they would, and we will, extend the ministry that He did while on earth. Can you imagine what the impact on the world would be if all believers began using their supernatural power through their identity in Christ?

Final Thoughts

When the Lord gave me the mandate to write this book, He placed on my heart how so many of us are missing the mark of following Jesus Christ and His teachings. I have talked to many people who do not know the promises of God in Scripture. Many of them attend church regularly, but they do not know their identity in God. They lack knowledge and wisdom on how to use the power and authority He has given them to overcome every obstacle they face in life. Many of us want to help lead others to Christ, but we cannot point them to salvation if we do not know the way through the Word.

We need to be taught God's Word so that we can enjoy the fullness of our lives with Him. This means taking great joy in everything – our faith, our family, our jobs, our friends – because we are doing everything to the glory of God. Jesus said that He came that we might have life and have it more abundantly. He is soon to come back. I know preachers have been saying this for many, many years, but I feel that with all the despair, hatred and destruction that we are currently witnessing in the world that Jesus will return soon. I always pray that none of us will be lost and that we follow the obedience of God through the teachings of His Word. God loves us so much!

Lord, I want to thank You for asking me to write this identity crisis book. I ask You, Lord, to inspire everyone who reads it. May it stir them up to find the true identity of You. I believe that Your power will embrace them with the truth of Your Word so when they pray they will see that the enemy is not more powerful than Jesus Christ, and they will start agreeing with their true identity of You within themselves.

May God ever bless you, and I pray that you will come to know Him personally so that His everlasting love and joy overflows in your life!

Reference

Life Application Study Bible. King James Version, 2nd ed.,

Tyndale House, 1997.

Index

Index

If you would like to contact Overseer Sandra D. Carter for prayer, you may visit Vision of Breath with Life Ministries at https://www.vobwlm.com/your-prayer-request. God has been using Overseer Carter through a powerful, prophetic ministry to help people find their identity through the Word of God.

www.ingramcontent.com/pod-product-compliance
Lightning Source LLC
Chambersburg PA
CBHW032026040426
42448CB00006B/736